The Unseen

Copyright © 2024 by A.J. Solano

All rights reserved. No part of this book may be reproduced in any manner whatsoever without written permission except in the case of brief quotations embodied in critical articles and reviews.

First Printing, 2024

The Unseen

Tales of Hidden Fears

A.J. Solano

Anthology

CONTENTS

INTRODUCTION xiii

1 | The Witness 1

The Unyielding Advocate

Echoes of the Past

The Unraveling

The Verdict of Shadows

2 | The Pod 11

The Comfort of Confinement

The Whisper of Fear

The Reluctant Awakening

The First Step

The New Beginning

3 | The Ghost in the Hallways 22

CONTENTS

The Silence

Tales of the Past

Storm of the Soul

The Faithful Night

The Silent Fade

4 | Eternal Youth in Influence 32

The Comment

The Mask

The Unseen Reflection

The Unfiltered

The New Dawn

5 | The Ascent of Fear 43

CONTENTS

The Promise of Heights

Unveiling the Fear

The Descent Into Dread

Confronting the Abyss

The Triumph Over Terror

6 | The Unseen Thirteenth   54

The Unseen Thirteenth

The Gathering

The Unraveling

The Thirteenth Hour

The Embrace

7 | the Stillness   64

CONTENTS

The Unsettling Silence

Vivid Silence

The hidden Presence

The Breaking Point

The Inescapable Truth

8 | In the Embrace of Flames   74

The Legacy of Ash

The Flames

The Heart of Fear

Into the Inferno

Resurrection from Ashes

9 | Silent Terrors in the Deep   84

The Ominous Message

10 | Avalanche   87

CONTENTS

The Ascent

The Resort

The Descent

The Burial

The Survival

11 | Veil of the Unseen Needle   98

The Announcement

The Escalation

The Breaking Point

The Invisible Enemy

A Glimmer of Hope

12 | The Cloud of Success   108

CONTENTS

The Inheritance

Th Gilded Cage

The Memories

The Breaking Point

The Embrace

13 | Kaleidoscope of Terror 118

The Vibrant Prison

Reflections of Fear

The Heart of the Maze

Fading into Silence

14 | The Storm 126

The Forsaken Shore

The Woods

Eyes Not Seen

The Signal in the Sky

The Heart of the Island

15 | The Creeping Agony 138

CONTENTS

The Awakening of Pain

The Relentless Pursuer

The Fall

The Decision

CONFRONTING FEARS: A JOURNEY TOWARDS BETTER MENTAL HEALTH 147

INTRODUCTION

In the shadowed corners of the mind, where fear whispers and doubt lingers, there lies a realm uncharted by reason. "The Unseen: Tales of Hidden Fears" is an anthology that ventures into this obscure territory, exploring the eerie landscape of our deepest anxieties. Each story in this collection is a window into the invisible terrors that haunt us - fears not spoken, but deeply felt, shaping our lives in ways we seldom understand.

These tales are not mere ghost stories or legends of the supernatural. They are reflections of the true horror that resides within us all - the unseen fears that pulse beneath the facade of normalcy. Set against the backdrop of our everyday world, these narratives twist the mundane into the macabre, revealing the unsettling truth that what we fear most may not be in the shadows, but within ourselves.

As you turn these pages, prepare to confront the unseen. You will meet characters caught in the grip of unnamable dread, their ordinary lives unraveled by the intangible. Through rich, evocative language, each story weaves a tapestry of tension and suspense, inviting you to glimpse the unspoken horrors that lie just out of sight.

Welcome to "The Unseen: Tales of Hidden Fears" - a journey into the heart of our darkest, most elusive fears. Let the journey begin.

1

The Witness

The Unyielding Advocate

In the heart of the city, where the skyline pierced the heavens with its steel spires, there existed a realm ruled not by kings or queens, but by the letter of the law. At the pinnacle of this realm stood Jonathan Hales, a lawyer whose reputation was as immaculate as the marble floors of the courthouse. Jonathan was a master of his craft, a weaver of words, turning juries with his silver tongue as easily as turning pages in a book. However, beneath this facade of invincibility lurked an insidious fear, a dread so potent it colored every victory and shadowed every triumph – the fear of failure.

His office, a high-rise chamber overlooking the city, was filled with the spoils of his success. Awards adorned the walls like trophies of war, each one a testament to his unbroken string of victories. But for Jonathan, they were not symbols of pride; they were reminders of the precipice upon which he perpetually stood. The fear of a single loss, a solitary failure, was a specter that haunted his every waking moment.

It was this very fear that drove him to lengths others might find morally ambiguous. Jonathan saved clients with the skill of a surgeon, meticulous and precise, even when he knew they were guilty. Every case was a battle against his own potential downfall, a war waged not in the realm of ethics but in the dominion of his own psyche.

One autumn evening, as amber hues bled into the city sky, Jonathan found himself in the familiar confines of his office, poring over case files. His newest client, a man of considerable influence accused of a heinous crime, was yet another test of his unblemished record. As Jonathan sifted through the evidence, meticulously planning his defense, an unsettling feeling crept over him. It was a sensation he had come to know too well – the gnawing doubt, the fear of an inevitable blemish on his perfect record.

But this case was different. Among the prosecution's list of witnesses was a name that made Jonathan's blood run cold. It was a name he recognized, not from legal directories or previous cases, but from a darker chapter of his own life. This witness, it seemed, was not just a mere participant in the trial but a harbinger of a past Jonathan had desperately tried to bury.

As the night deepened, the city lights flickering like distant stars, Jonathan sat motionless, the files spread before him now seemingly insurmountable. The witness's name echoed in his mind, a relentless tide eroding the fortress he had built around his fears. For the first time, Jonathan felt the unshakeable grip of a possibility he had never entertained – the possibility of a downfall, not at the hands of his own failings, but at the behest of a ghost from his past.

Echoes of the Past

As dawn broke over the city, casting a pale light on its towering edifices, Jonathan Hales found himself in the grip of a sleepless night. The specter of the upcoming trial, particularly the presence of the mysterious witness, had ensnared his thoughts, turning them into a labyrinth of anxiety and dread.

In his office, the early morning light did little to dispel the shadows that seemed to cling to the walls, as if they were manifestations of Jonathan's own fears. He had always known that the path he tread was fraught with moral ambiguity, but the fear of failure had always been a more immediate, more pressing concern than the distant whisper of conscience.

The witness, whose name resonated with echoes of a past Jonathan had tried to forget, was more than just a threat to his professional record. This person was a remnant of a time when Jonathan, still a fledgling lawyer, had made choices that now haunted him. It was a time when his fear of failure was just taking root, a time when he had bent the law in ways that now threatened to come back and shatter his carefully constructed world.

As he prepared for the day, Jonathan's mind raced with possibilities. Who was this witness? How were they connected to his past, and what knowledge did they hold that could unravel his present? These questions spun a web of paranoia that tightened around him, making every step feel like a descent into a trap of his own making.

Arriving at the courthouse, Jonathan felt as if he were walking into a different realm. The hallowed halls, with their echoes of justice and order, seemed to mock his inner turmoil. The trial was set to begin, and as the courtroom filled, Jonathan scanned the faces, searching for the one that had kept him awake all night.

When the witness finally entered, a chill ran down Jonathan's spine. It wasn't just recognition that struck him, but a sense of inevitability. The witness's eyes met his, and in that moment, Jonathan knew that this trial was not like the others. This was a reckoning.

As the proceedings began, Jonathan listened with a facade of calm professionalism, but inside, he was wrestling with a storm of emotions. The witness's testimony was precise, their memory unyielding, and with each word, Jonathan felt the walls of his fortress of success begin to crack.

By the time the court adjourned for the day, Jonathan was a portrait of composed agony. The evidence was damning, the witness credible, and his client's guilt seemed all but assured. But it was not the prospect of losing the case that tormented Jonathan the most; it was the realization that his past, a past he had thought buried, was resurrecting, bringing with it a darkness that threatened to consume not just his career, but his very soul.

The Unraveling

The courtroom had become a crucible, with each day of the trial adding to the heat that threatened to melt away Jonathan's façade. The witness, unrelenting in their testimony, seemed to be the embodiment of all his fears – a living reminder of a path once taken, a choice made in desperation.

Outside the courtroom, the city moved with its usual rhythm, oblivious to the drama unfolding within its judicial heart. But for Jonathan, the city felt different now; its tall buildings seemed like sentinels watching his every move, its bustling streets a maze designed to confuse and confound him.

As the trial progressed, Jonathan found himself increasingly isolated. His colleagues, sensing the shift in the winds, kept a wary distance. His clients, once confident in his abilities, now whispered doubts and concerns. But it was the solitude within that was most suffocating. His fear of failure, once a driving force, had become a paralyzing agent, freezing him in a moment of perpetual uncertainty.

Each night, Jonathan returned to his apartment, a luxurious space that now felt like a gilded cage. The walls, adorned with his legal achievements, seemed to mock him with their silent judgment. Sleep, when it came, brought no respite, only dreams haunted by shadows and whispers of his past.

The turning point came unexpectedly. On a day that began like any other, a piece of evidence was introduced that changed everything. It was a document, a seemingly innocuous piece of paper, but to Jonathan, it was a ghost from his past life. The document, a record of a decision he had made years ago, was the missing link that connected him to the crime for which his client now stood accused.

In that moment, as the prosecution presented the document to the court, Jonathan felt the ground beneath him shift. The walls of the courtroom seemed to close in, the air grew thin, and the faces of the jury blurred into a sea of judgment. His heart raced, his mind reeled, and the fear that had been his constant companion now screamed in triumph.

The rest of the day passed in a blur. Jonathan's defense was a shadow of its usual brilliance, his arguments hollow and unconvincing. The jury, once swayed by his eloquence, now looked upon him with suspicion and doubt.

That evening, as Jonathan sat alone in his office, the full weight of his situation descended upon him. His career, his reputation, everything he had worked for, was unraveling before his eyes. The fear of failure had become a self-fulfilling prophecy, a dark narrative that he had written with his own actions.

As the city lights flickered outside his window, Jonathan realized that the trial was no longer about his client, nor was it about the witness or the crime. It was about him – his past, his choices, and the inevitable reckoning that comes when one builds a life on a foundation of fear.

The Verdict of Shadows

The final day of the trial arrived with a somber air. Jonathan Hales, once the embodiment of confidence and legal acumen, now walked the corridors of the courthouse like a ghost, haunted by the specter of his impending downfall.

The courtroom was packed, a hive of murmured speculation and anticipation. Jonathan's client, who had once looked at him as a savior, now offered only a glare of betrayal and fear. The jury, those arbiters of fate, returned to their seats, their expressions unreadable, their verdict a sealed enigma.

As the proceedings began, Jonathan felt detached, as if he were a spectator in his own life's drama. The fear that had once driven him now seemed distant, replaced by a resignation to whatever fate awaited him. His eyes frequently met the witness's, searching for a hint of malice or satisfaction, but found only a calm indifference.

When the moment came for the jury to deliver their verdict, a hush fell over the courtroom. The foreman rose, and as he spoke the words "Guilty," it was as though time slowed. Each syllable echoed in Jonathan's ears, a death knell to his career, his reputation, his very identity.

In the aftermath, as the courtroom erupted into a cacophony of reactions, Jonathan remained motionless, lost in a maelstrom of emotions. The conviction of his client was a foregone conclusion, yet it was not this that weighed most heavily on him. It was the realization that his relentless pursuit of victory, driven by his fear of failure, had been his undoing.

The days that followed were a blur. Jonathan's once bright career dimmed, overshadowed by the scandal and the whispers of his peers. His victories, once sources of pride, now seemed hollow, tainted by the knowledge of what they had cost him.

In a final act of reckoning, Jonathan decided to confront the witness, seeking closure if not absolution. The meeting, away from the prying eyes of the media and the legal community, was a quiet affair. The witness, no longer a faceless entity in the narrative of his downfall, was revealed to be more than just a conduit of his past; they were a mirror reflecting the consequences of his choices.

Their conversation was not one of accusations or forgiveness, but of understanding. The witness spoke of their own journey, of choices made and paths taken, not so different from Jonathan's. It was a revelation that, in their own way, everyone was a prisoner of their fears, some just had more visible shackles.

As Jonathan left the meeting, the burden he carried felt lighter, not because his situation had changed, but because his perspective had. The fear of failure, which had once dominated his life, had lost its grip on him. In its place was a newfound understanding of the complex tapestry of human motivation and frailty.

The story of Jonathan Hales did not end in triumph or redemption, but in a quiet acceptance of the flawed nature of ambition and the inexorable truth that sometimes, our greatest fears are the architects of our destiny.

2

The Pod

The Comfort of Confinement

I've always found solace in the confined spaces of my pod. It's a sanctuary, a world where the gentle hum of technology synchronizes with the rhythm of my heartbeat. The world outside, a vast expanse of uncertainty, has never been part of my reality. Why venture out when the drones bring everything to my doorstep? Food, clothes, even the synthetic scents of what they say the outside world smells like. My job, my friends, my entire existence — all experienced through the safe, predictable lens of virtual reality.

But today, something is amiss. The screens flicker, a static buzz replaces the usual clarity of my virtual meeting room. Faces of my colleagues distort into pixelated masks of confusion. And then, darkness. A silence that's deafening. The virtual world, my world, has been unplugged.

The Whisper of Fear

Panic claws at my chest as I realize the gravity of the situation. A cyber attack, they say. The AI, our trusted ally in this self-contained existence, has turned on us. I try to call someone, anyone, but the network is dead. The realization hits me like a wave of icy water — I am utterly alone.

The thought of stepping outside my pod, into the real world, sends shivers down my spine. I've heard stories, myths almost, about the 'outside.' A place of chaos, unpredictability, a vast open space that swallows you whole. My breath quickens, my palms sweat. The very idea of exposing myself to that endless void is paralyzing.

The Reluctant Awakening

Days pass. My supplies dwindle. The comforting cocoon of my pod feels more like a prison now. Hunger gnaws at me, both for food and for a connection, any connection, to another human soul. The silence is oppressive, a constant reminder of my isolation.

In a moment of desperation, I approach the pod's exit. My hand hovers over the release button. I close my eyes, images of the infinite outside swirling in my mind. The fear is a tangible thing, wrapping its icy fingers around my throat. But beneath the fear, there's a spark, a tiny ember of curiosity. What is out there, beyond the safety of my pod?

The First Step

With a trembling hand, I press the button. The door hisses open, and for the first time, I step out. The world is not what I expected. It's quieter, more serene. The vastness of the sky, a tapestry of blues and grays, is overwhelming yet oddly mesmerizing.

I walk, each step a battle against the screaming instinct to run back to my pod. The outside world is not a gaping void but a canvas of endless possibilities. I see remnants of the old world, structures overrun by nature, a testament to humanity's forgotten footprint.

The New Beginning

I've faced my deepest fear, not just of the outside, but of the unknown. The cyber attack, a curse in disguise, forced me out of my shell. In this new world, I find strength in my vulnerability, a sense of freedom in the uncharted paths before me. The fear still lingers, a shadow in my peripheral vision, but it no longer controls me.

As I stand under the open sky, I realize that life is more than just existing. It's about stepping into the unknown, embracing the vastness with open arms. Maybe, just maybe, this is the start of something beautiful — a life lived beyond the confines of a pod.

3

The Ghost in the Hallways

The Silence

In the quiet town of Eagle's Nest, nestled between rolling hills and ancient pines, there was a high school that stood as a beacon of routine and normalcy. But for Jayden, a Native American teenager with deep brown eyes that seemed to carry the weight of the world, school was anything but normal.

Jayden moved through the crowded hallways like a ghost, his presence barely acknowledged, his words seldom spoken. His peers, a blur of faces and voices, were like an ocean in which he felt he was perpetually drowning. He wore a constant mask of indifference, but inside, his heart raced with an unnameable dread at the mere thought of interaction.

His fear wasn't of people themselves but of the judgments, the expectations, the unknown thoughts that might lurk behind their smiles or frowns. It was as if every gaze held a whisper of a threat, every laugh a hidden barb. He found solace only in the corners of the library, amidst books that spoke in hushed tones and asked for nothing in return.

Tales of the Past

Jayden's father, a proud man of the Navajo tribe, often spoke of the importance of community and connection. He told stories of ancestors who thrived on unity and mutual support. But to Jayden, these tales felt like echoes from a distant past, unreachable and alien.

At school, his teachers saw potential in him, his sharp mind and keen insights during the rare moments he chose to speak. But they also saw the walls he built around himself, invisible yet impenetrable. Attempts to draw him out often resulted in further retreat, a retreat into a world where he felt safe but terribly alone.

Storm of the Soul

The school announced a mandatory social event, a gathering meant to foster community spirit. For Jayden, the news came like a storm cloud looming on the horizon. His classmates buzzed with excitement, plans forming, groups merging. For them, it was a chance to shine, to connect. For Jayden, it was a nightmare taking shape.

As the day approached, his sleep became haunted by dreams of suffocating crowds, of voices melding into a cacophony that left him breathless. He began to withdraw even more, his responses in class dwindling to nods or shakes of the head, his eyes constantly seeking escape routes.

The Faithful Night

The night of the event, the school gym was transformed into a whirl of colors and sounds. Jayden stood at the periphery, his back to the wall, watching the scene with a sense of impending doom. He felt eyes on him, imagined whispers weaving through the crowd. He wanted to run, to escape to his safe haven of books and solitude.

Then, an unexpected hand on his shoulder, a classmate trying to draw him into the dance. Panic surged through Jayden, a tidal wave that swept away reason. He pushed away, his movement too forceful, sending his classmate crashing into a nearby table.

The music stopped. All eyes turned to him, a collective gaze that felt like a thousand needles. The whispers he always feared seemed to become real, a chorus of judgment that filled the gym. Jayden ran, ran through the halls, out of the school, into the darkening night.

The Silent Fade

They found Jayden the next morning, lying still at the base of an ancient pine. The coroner said it was a heart attack, rare but not unheard of in teenagers under severe stress. The school mourned, teachers and students alike speaking in hushed tones about the quiet boy who had always seemed so distant.

In the weeks that followed, his desk sat empty, a silent testament to the struggle that had gone unseen, the fear that had been too deep, too overwhelming to voice. Jayden's father stood at the edge of the school grounds, looking at the building that had been both a battleground and a refuge for his son. In his heart, he knew the stories of unity and connection would now carry a whisper of a different kind, a reminder of the unseen shadows that can dwell in the human heart.

4

Eternal Youth in Influence

The Comment

The glow of my phone was the only light in my otherwise dark room. It was past midnight, and the world outside was silent, but in the digital realm, my life was relentlessly buzzing. As a social media influencer, my existence was a kaleidoscope of likes, shares, and comments. Every post was a carefully curated slice of perfection, a testament to the vibrant, youthful image I had cultivated over the years.

But tonight, as I scrolled through the sea of positivity, a single comment caught my eye and made my heart stop. "Looks like age is finally catching up with her," it read. Just a few words, but they struck like a viper's bite.

I felt a cold shiver run down my spine as I read and reread the comment. I had always known that aging was inevitable, but in the world I inhabited, youth was the currency of relevance. My entire career, my identity, hinged on the perception of eternal youthfulness.

I rushed to the mirror, my heart pounding in my ears. The reflection staring back at me was familiar, yet in that moment, it felt like a stranger's face. Were those lines around my eyes always there? Was my skin always this dull? The questions spiraled, each one feeding my growing panic.

The room felt smaller, the walls closing in. It was as if time itself was accelerating, each tick of the clock a reminder of my inevitable descent into obscurity. The fear was visceral, gripping me with an intensity that left me breathless. I was trapped in a relentless tide, pulling me away from the shores of youth, towards an unknown, terrifying future.

In the depths of that night, alone with my reflection and the haunting echo of that comment, I felt an abyss open within me. A profound dread of losing not just my youth, but everything it represented – my identity, my relevance, my very existence in the digital world I called home.

The fear was more than just a fear of aging; it was a fear of becoming invisible in a world that only celebrated the perpetual bloom of youth.

The Mask

The next morning, I awoke to a reality I could no longer ignore. The comment from last night echoed in my mind, a relentless reminder of my deepest fear. I stared at my reflection, my eyes tracing every line, every imperfection. The vibrant, confident persona I projected to the world felt like a distant memory.

I sat at my vanity, surrounded by an arsenal of cosmetics, each promising the illusion of unblemished youth. As I applied makeup, I realized I was crafting a mask, a facade to hide behind. Each stroke was a desperate attempt to preserve the image I had so carefully built, to hold onto the identity that had brought me adoration, success, and a sense of belonging.

But the mask felt heavier today. The layers of foundation and concealer couldn't hide the dread gnawing at my soul. The more I tried to conceal my fears, the more suffocating they became. I was caught in a paradox – the very thing that brought me fame was now the source of my deepest insecurity.

Throughout the day, as I posed for photos and interacted with my followers, a part of me felt detached, as if I was watching someone else live my life. The vibrant colors of the photos, the lively emojis, the enthusiastic comments – they all felt like echoes from a different world, a world where I no longer belonged.

With each notification, my heart raced, fearing another comment that would shatter the illusion I was clinging to. I realized that my fear of aging wasn't just about losing my looks; it was about losing my relevance, my place in a world that idolized the fleeting beauty of youth.

As night fell, I found myself once again alone in the darkness, the light from my phone casting shadows across the room. The mask I wore for the world was gone, and all that was left was the raw, unfiltered truth of my fear.

In the silence, I understood the irony – in my pursuit of eternal youth, I had lost the essence of who I was. My identity had become a prisoner to the fear of becoming invisible, lost in the relentless march of time.

The realization was both terrifying and liberating. I knew that the journey ahead would be fraught with challenges, but for the first time, I felt a flicker of hope. Perhaps there was more to my existence than the superficial allure of eternal youth. Perhaps it was time to embrace the inevitable changes and find a new path, one where my worth wasn't defined by the number of likes or the smoothness of my skin.

But as I pondered this new path, the fear lingered, a shadowy specter in the corner of my mind, whispering doubts and uncertainties.

The Unseen Reflection

That night, I did something I hadn't done in years. I turned off my phone, silencing the endless barrage of notifications. The room was quiet, a stark contrast to the constant noise of my online existence. It was just me, alone with my thoughts, away from the prying eyes of the world.

I stood before my mirror again, but this time, it was different. I wiped off the layers of makeup, revealing the face I had hidden from both the world and myself. The face in the mirror was me – not the influencer, not the icon, but the raw, unadorned person I had long neglected.

As I gazed into my own eyes, a surge of emotions washed over me. I saw the fear, the vulnerability, but also a glimmer of something else – a strength that had been buried under the weight of expectations and the fear of obsolescence.

In that moment, a realization dawned upon me. My fear of aging wasn't just about my appearance; it was about losing control. In a world where I curated every post, every image, every aspect of my life, the inevitability of aging was the one thing I couldn't manipulate or disguise. It was a reminder of my own humanity, my own mortality.

For hours, I sat there, reflecting on the years I had spent chasing an ideal that was both unattainable and transient. I thought of all the moments I had missed, too caught up in portraying a life of perpetual youth and perfection. The real moments, the ones that truly mattered, were lost in the pursuit of likes and follows.

As dawn broke, a sense of calm enveloped me. I realized that while I couldn't stop time, I could change my relationship with it. Instead of fearing each passing day, I could embrace it as an opportunity to grow, to learn, to evolve.

I turned on my phone again, but this time, with a new perspective. I decided to share a post unlike any I had shared before – a photo of my true self, without filters, without makeup, without the facade. It was a declaration of my willingness to face my fear, to step out of the shadows of eternal youth and into the light of authenticity.

The response was overwhelming. Messages of support, admiration, and even relief flooded in. It seemed that in revealing my vulnerability, I had connected with my followers on a level deeper than I ever had with my carefully curated content.

In that moment, I found a new kind of freedom – the freedom to be imperfect, to be real, to be human. I had stepped into a new chapter of my life, one where the unseen reflection in the mirror was no longer a source of fear, but a testament to a life lived authentically and courageously.

The Unfiltered

The days following my unfiltered post felt like walking through a new world. I no longer woke up with a sense of dread, fearing the march of time. Instead, I embraced each morning with a curiosity I hadn't felt since I was a young girl, unburdened by the glare of the spotlight.

My social media feed, once a meticulously curated gallery, began to reflect the real me. I shared moments of joy, moments of struggle, moments of introspection. With each post, I peeled back the layers I had built over the years, revealing the multifaceted person I was beneath the influencer persona.

But change, even positive change, comes with its own set of challenges. Not everyone was pleased with the new direction I was taking. Some followers yearned for the old, glamorous images, the eternal beacon of youth I once represented. Their comments, steeped in disappointment, were a reminder of the transient nature of online adoration.

Despite this, I pressed on, fueled by a newfound purpose. I realized that my journey was not just about confronting my fear of aging, but about redefining what it meant to be an influencer. I wanted to inspire not just through beauty and perfection, but through authenticity and resilience.

As I shared more of my true self, I began to connect with my followers on a deeper level. Their messages were no longer just about my looks or my lifestyle. They shared their own fears, their own struggles, their own journeys towards self-acceptance. It was as if by facing my own fear, I had given them permission to face theirs.

However, the most profound change was within me. I started to see the beauty in the little things, the everyday moments that I had once overlooked. I found joy in the laugh lines that appeared when I smiled, the stories they told of a life filled with laughter and love.

One evening, as I sat watching the sunset, I realized how much my perception of time had changed. It was no longer an enemy, a relentless force to be feared and fought against. It was a companion, a measure of the experiences that shaped me, the journey that molded me.

I understood then that true influence wasn't about projecting an image of eternal youth, but about embracing the echoes of time – the wisdom, the growth, the authenticity that comes with the passing years.

In that beautiful, fleeting moment, watching the sky shift from orange to purple, I felt at peace. I was no longer chasing the shadows of eternal youth. Instead, I was living in the light of my truth, resonant with the echoes of time.

The New Dawn

Months had passed since I embarked on this journey of self-discovery and acceptance. The fear that once consumed me, the terror of aging and losing my place in the digital world, had transformed into a source of strength and inspiration.

My social media presence had evolved dramatically. It was no longer just about showcasing a life of glamour and youth. Instead, it became a platform for genuine expression, for sharing the ups and downs of life, the beauty of aging, and the wisdom gained through experience.

I had started using my influence to advocate for a more authentic portrayal of life in the digital age. I spoke about the pressures of maintaining a perfect image, the unrealistic standards set by the media, and the importance of self-love and acceptance. My message resonated with people of all ages, transcending the superficial boundaries of beauty and youth.

The impact of this shift was profound. I received countless messages from followers who felt empowered by my honesty. They shared their own stories of overcoming fears, of embracing their true selves, and of finding joy in the journey of life.

As I reflected on my own journey, I realized how much I had grown. The young woman who feared aging had matured into someone who appreciated the depth and richness of life. I had learned to value the wisdom that comes with age, to cherish the memories etched in every line and wrinkle.

One crisp morning, as I walked through the park, I noticed the leaves changing colors, a reminder of the beauty in change and the cycle of life. It struck me that aging was similar – a natural, beautiful process, a testament to a life lived fully.

I stopped to take a picture, not to post online, but for myself. A keepsake of this moment, a symbol of my newfound perspective. The sunlight filtering through the leaves cast a warm, golden glow, mirroring the light I felt inside.

As I looked around, I saw the world with new eyes. I saw people of all ages, each with their own story, their own journey. It was a tapestry of human experience, rich and diverse, and I was a part of it.

The fear that once seemed like an insurmountable mountain was now just a distant memory. In its place was a sense of gratitude for each day, for the opportunity to grow, to learn, to experience the full spectrum of life.

I returned home, feeling a sense of fulfillment and peace. I sat down to write a post, not as an influencer, but as a fellow traveler on this journey of life. I wrote about the beauty of aging, the grace in accepting change, and the joy in living authentically.

As I hit 'post', I knew that this was just the beginning of a new chapter. A chapter where age was not a fear to be conquered, but a badge of honor to be celebrated. A new dawn had arrived, and I was ready to embrace it with open arms and an open heart.

5

The Ascent of Fear

The Promise of Heights

The sun had begun its slow descent behind the rugged peaks of Zion National Park, casting elongated shadows across the narrow pathway of Angel's Landing. Evelyn and Michael, hand in hand, had ventured far beyond the well-trodden trails, seeking a private sanctuary for their special moment. Michael's heart raced with anticipation, not just for the proposal he planned but also for the thrill of adventure that always accompanied their escapades.

As they navigated through a less trodden path, lush with wildflowers and the occasional curious chipmunk, the couple reveled in the solitude. They were adventurers at heart, always seeking the next thrill, the next beautiful vista. But as they approached their destination, a secluded overlook with a breathtaking view, an unspoken tension began to build.

Unveiling the Fear

The overlook was stunning, a precarious ledge offering a panoramic view of the valley below. Michael, with a confident smile, stepped closer to the edge, beckoning Evelyn to join him. But as Evelyn approached, her steps faltered. The vast expanse of space, the sheer drop just a footstep away, sent a visceral shiver through her body.

She had always known about her discomfort with heights, but in the excitement of their adventures, she had managed to keep it at bay. Now, faced with the gaping chasm below, her fear manifested in full force. Her heart pounded in her chest, her palms grew clammy, and a dizzying sense of vertigo threatened to overwhelm her.

Michael, sensing her hesitation, reached out a comforting hand. "It's okay," he whispered, mistaking her fear for simple nervousness. "It's just us here, in this beautiful world."

The Descent Into Dread

The proposal, though heartfelt and tearfully accepted, was overshadowed by the looming challenge of their return. As they retraced their steps, the narrowness of the path, which had seemed adventurous on their way up, now felt menacing. Every rock and root was a potential trip hazard, every gust of wind a malicious force.

Evelyn's breaths came in short, sharp gasps. The ground seemed to sway beneath her feet. The vastness of the sky above and the depth of the valley below converged, creating a spinning tunnel around her. Michael, attuned to her growing panic, tried to offer words of comfort, but they were lost in the whirlwind of her fear.

Confronting the Abyss

They reached a particularly narrow section, a mere ribbon of earth wedged between the abyss and the unyielding rock face. Evelyn froze, unable to move forward, her mind replaying horrific visions of slipping, falling, tumbling into the void.

Michael, his own heart pounding with a mix of fear and concern, gently coaxed her. "Look at me, Evelyn. Focus on me. We'll take this one step at a time."

With trembling legs and a resolve born out of necessity, Evelyn edged forward, her gaze locked on Michael. Each step was a battle against her instincts screaming at her to retreat, to escape the exposed heights.

The Triumph Over Terror

As they finally emerged onto safer, wider ground, the couple collapsed in each other's arms, a mix of relief and exhaustion washing over them. The sun had set, and in the twilight, the world seemed a little less daunting.

Evelyn, still shaken but imbued with a newfound strength, looked up into Michael's eyes. "I never knew I could be so scared and yet so alive," she whispered.

Their descent from Angel's Landing was more than just a physical journey; it was a voyage through the landscape of fear, a testament to the power of love and courage in the face of the unknown.

6

The Unseen Thirteenth

The Unseen Thirteenth

In the heart of a bustling city, where the streets thrummed with life and light, there lived a man named Arthur. To the outside world, he was an epitome of success – a well-respected banker, esteemed by his peers, admired for his impeccable logic and rationality. Yet, Arthur harbored a secret, a fear so deeply ingrained that it shadowed his every step, unseen but ever-present.

Arthur's world was meticulously ordered, a bastion against the chaos he dreaded. His life was a series of calculated steps, a routine unmarred by unpredictability. But there was one thing that Arthur couldn't control, something that made his heart race and palms sweat – the number thirteen.

This fear was not just a mild superstition but a crippling phobia that infiltrated his existence. He lived on the twelfth floor, consciously avoiding the floor above. He would never make transactions involving the dreaded number, and even dates bearing this numeral were days of anxiety and unrest.

It began subtly, with the mere sight of the number causing discomfort. But, as days turned into months, and months into years, the fear grew, wrapping its icy fingers around his mind.

As Arthur sat in his office one chilly autumn morning, he received an invitation that sent a shiver down his spine. His firm was celebrating its thirteenth anniversary with a grand gala. The mere thought of attending an event honoring the number he dreaded was unthinkable. Yet, his position demanded his presence.

The Gathering

As the gala approached, Arthur's unease transformed into a suffocating dread. Sleep evaded him, replaced by nightmarish visions where the number thirteen loomed like a malevolent specter, warping his reality. His days were marred by anxiety, the once-clear boundaries of logic and reason blurring into the realms of the irrational.

Colleagues whispered, noticing Arthur's growing distress. Meetings were missed, projects delayed. The once-steadfast banker was now a shadow of his former self, haunted by an unseen, unspoken terror.'

The night of the gala arrived, a grand affair set in the heart of the city's most luxurious hotel. The venue was a hive of celebration, a stark contrast to the turmoil churning within Arthur. Stepping into the ornate ballroom, his eyes darted around, fixating on every instance of the number: table thirteen, thirteen steps leading to the stage, the clock striking thirteen minutes past the hour.

With each sighting, a cold shiver ran down his spine, his heart racing, his breaths shallow. The once-familiar faces of his colleagues seemed to twist into mocking grins, the laughter and music morphing into a cacophony that echoed the chaos in his mind.

The climax of the evening approached – the unveiling of a commemorative plaque. Arthur's heart sank as he realized the inevitable. The plaque bore the number: thirteen. It wasn't just a number anymore; it felt like a malevolent entity, mocking his attempts at control, threatening to shatter the fragile veneer of normalcy he had clung to.

The Unraveling

The days following the gala were a blur for Arthur. His mind, once a fortress of rationality, had become a labyrinth of shadows and whispers, each corner echoing with the dread of the number thirteen. The phobia had taken a corporeal form in his life, an inescapable presence that lurked in every moment, every decision.

Arthur's once impeccable professional reputation began to crumble. His superiors, concerned and perplexed by his erratic behavior, started questioning his capabilities. Friends and colleagues, who had once admired his analytical mind, now looked upon him with a mixture of pity and unease.

The turning point came on an ordinary Thursday. Arthur had meticulously avoided any task or meeting associated with the number, but fate, it seemed, had other plans. A crucial meeting was rescheduled to the thirteenth of the month, a day Arthur had always taken off as a sick day, a small act of defiance against his unseen adversary.

But this time, he couldn't escape. The meeting was with the firm's most important client, and his attendance was not just expected; it was mandatory. As the day approached, Arthur felt as though he were walking towards an abyss. The night before the meeting, sleep was a distant dream. His mind raced with a torrent of thoughts, each more terrifying than the last.

The Thirteenth Hour

On the day of the meeting, Arthur's world was a maelstrom of fear and panic. Every tick of the clock was a thunderous echo in his ears, counting down to the dreaded hour. He arrived at the office, his steps heavy, his heart a prisoner to the relentless march of time.

As he entered the meeting room, his eyes inadvertently caught the date on a colleague's phone. It was the thirteenth. The room seemed to spin, the faces around him melting into a sea of numbers, each morphing into the accursed thirteen.

The client arrived, and as the meeting commenced, Arthur's voice was barely a whisper, his thoughts fragmented by the overwhelming terror that consumed him. Words lost their meaning, numbers danced before his eyes, and the world reduced to a single, inescapable truth – he was in the grip of the thirteenth.

In a moment of sheer panic, Arthur stood up, his chair clattering to the floor. He mumbled an apology, his voice choked with fear, and rushed out of the room, leaving a trail of shocked and confused faces behind.

The Embrace

In the aftermath, Arthur's life was irrevocably altered. He took a leave of absence from work, retreating into the confines of his apartment, a sanctuary from the outside world and its unpredictable encounters with the number.

Here, in the solitude of his home, Arthur confronted the full extent of his phobia. It was no longer a distant fear, but a part of him, an unyielding shadow that had eclipsed his life. In this introspection, Arthur realized that his fear was not of the number itself, but of what it represented – chaos, unpredictability, the unknown.

The story concludes with Arthur beginning a slow, painful journey towards understanding and acceptance. He starts seeing a therapist, unraveling the layers of his phobia, confronting the deep-seated anxieties that fueled it. It's a journey not towards cure, but towards reconciliation – with his fears, with the unpredictability of life, and with himself.

7

the Stillness

The Unsettling Silence

In the dim light of my workshop, surrounded by the silent gazes of creatures once wild and free, I find a cold comfort. My hands, skilled in the art of taxidermy, move with a precision born of years of practice. Yet, as night falls, the stillness of my surroundings begins to weigh heavily on me. The unblinking eyes of my lifeless subjects seem to pierce through the gloom, and an unsettling feeling takes root in my heart.

My thoughts often drift to the inevitable - the cessation of life. It's an irony not lost on me, a taxidermist, who spends his days preserving the semblance of life in the deceased. But as the shadows grow longer, my mind fixates on the finality of death, the immutability of it. The mere idea sends shivers down my spine, and I find myself glancing over my shoulder, half-expecting to see something more than the lifeless figures that populate my workspace.

Vivid Silence

Nights have become a battleground of sleepless dread. Every creak of the old house, every rustle outside my window seems amplified, as if the quiet is speaking a language I dare not understand. In my dreams, I wander through an endless maze of rooms, each filled with the silent, accusing stares of animals I've worked on. They seem to be asking me something, but their voices are just whispers, lost in a wind I cannot feel.

I've started to avoid working late, the eerie stillness of the workshop becoming unbearable as dusk approaches. Even the tools of my trade, once comforting in their familiarity, now feel like accomplices to some unspeakable crime. The piercing of needle through skin, the gentle manipulation of lifeless limbs – each action is a reminder of the fragility of life and the certainty of its end.

The hidden Presence

It was a rainy evening when I first felt it. A presence in the room with me, something unseen but deeply felt. My heart raced as I looked around, half-expecting to see a ghostly figure among the stuffed foxes and birds. But there was nothing, only the sound of rain against the windows and the thunderous beating of my own heart.

I told myself it was just my imagination, a trick of the mind of someone who spends too much time with the dead. But the feeling persisted, growing stronger with each passing day. I began to rush through my work, eager to leave the oppressive atmosphere of the workshop. The once cherished solitude of my profession had become a source of unrelenting anxiety.

The Breaking Point

Last night, I reached my breaking point. As I was leaving the workshop, I heard a sound that froze me in my tracks – a soft, almost inaudible sigh. It seemed to come from everywhere and nowhere, a breath suspended in the still air. My hands trembled, and I could feel the cold sweat on my brow. I wanted to run, but my feet were rooted to the spot.

When I finally mustered the courage to turn on the light, the room was as I left it – quiet, still, lifeless. Yet the feeling of being watched, of being not alone, was overwhelming. I fled the workshop, locking the door behind me, my heart pounding in my ears.

The Inescapable Truth

Now, I sit in my living room, the morning light doing little to dispel the fear that clings to me. I realize that my phobia, this deep-seated fear of death and decay, is not just about the dead. It's about the reminder they carry – that life is transient, that we are all, in the end, destined for the same stillness.

I know I cannot escape this truth, just as I cannot escape the shadows that seem to linger in the corners of my vision. Perhaps it's time to confront this fear, to face the whispers in the stillness head-on. But as I stand up, preparing to return to my workshop, I can't shake the feeling that something awaits me there, something as real as my fear, hidden in the guise of shadows and silence.

8

In the Embrace of Flames

The Legacy of Ash

In a small, rain-soaked town, where the fog often clung to the streets like a lingering whisper, there lived a young man named Ethan. His father, a revered firefighter, had perished in a blaze that tore through the heart of the town years ago. Since then, Ethan, with eyes like smoldering coals and a heart heavy with unspoken grief, had stepped into his father's oversized boots, donning the very uniform that once symbolized heroism but now felt like a shroud of haunting memories.

The firehouse, a place once filled with laughter and tales of bravery, now echoed with the silent weight of his father's absence. Ethan moved through his days like a shadow, training relentlessly, driven by a duty that was as much a curse as it was a calling. The other firefighters respected his skill but were wary of the somber intensity that never left his gaze.

The Flames

One fateful night, as the town slept, a distress call shattered the stillness. A fire, wild and unforgiving, had erupted at the old mill. As the fire engines screamed through the deserted streets, Ethan's heart raced with a familiar dread. The roaring flames beckoned him, their crackling voices whispering of his deepest fear and darkest night.

Arriving at the inferno, Ethan's breath hitched. The fire danced with a malevolent grace, its tongues licking the sky, painting it in shades of terror. His fellow firefighters sprang into action, but Ethan stood frozen, the ghost of his father's fate flickering in the furious blaze before him.

The Heart of Fear

Ethan's captain, a grizzled veteran with eyes that had seen too many battles against nature's fury, placed a firm hand on his shoulder. "Ethan, we need you. Your father would have charged in without a second thought." But those words, meant to inspire, only tightened the cold grip of fear around Ethan's heart.

As the team fought to contain the blaze, Ethan's mind was engulfed in a different kind of fire – one that burned from within, scorching his resolve and fueling his terror. Memories of his father, strong and invincible, being consumed by the very element he sought to conquer, played in an endless loop in Ethan's mind.

Into the Inferno

With a sudden, almost supernatural effort, Ethan shook off the paralyzing dread. He knew he couldn't let his fear, his pyrophobia, dictate his destiny. Masking his face against the smoke and heat, he plunged into the heart of the flames.

Inside, the world was an orchestra of fire, a cacophony of destruction that threatened to overwhelm his senses. But as he moved, methodically, almost mechanically, to rescue those trapped inside, a strange calm settled over him. In confronting his fear, he found a flicker of courage, an ember of his father's legacy.

Resurrection from Ashes

As dawn broke, the fire was vanquished, leaving behind only the charred remains of what once was. Ethan emerged from the ruins, his face streaked with soot, his eyes no longer smoldering with fear but glowing with a newfound resolve.

He had faced his demon, not extinguished it, but learned to coexist with it. In the ashes of the old mill, Ethan found not just the remnants of a fire conquered but the rebirth of his own spirit, forever changed, forever scarred, but unbroken.

9

Silent Terrors in the Deep

The Ominous Message

11:30 PM - Alex's Phone

[News Alert]: *Breaking News: Local Water Supply Reportedly Contaminated - Authorities Investigating*

Alex: *(to Jordan)* Did you see this news alert?
Jordan: Yeah, just now. Contaminated how?
Alex: No details yet. Just says "investigating."
Jordan: Probably just a scare. Happens all the time.
Alex: I don't know, man. What if it's serious?

Next Morning - Alex's Kitchen

Alex: *(to himself)* Don't drink the water. Don't drink the water.
Alex's Phone Beeps
[Mom]: Morning, honey. Remember to stay hydrated!
Alex: *(typing hesitantly)* About that, mom...
[Mom]: Something wrong?
Alex: There was a warning about the water.
[Mom]: Just boil it, dear. It'll be fine.
Alex: *(staring at the tap)* But what if it's not?

Later That Day - At Work

Alex: *(to Jordan)* Everyone's talking about the water.
Jordan: *(typing)* It's just a precaution, Alex.

Alex: But what if it's something... carcinogenic?
Jordan: You're worrying too much.
Alex: *(types, then deletes)* What if we're all in danger?

Alex's heart pounds as he looks around, seeing colleagues drinking bottled water, whispering
.

That Evening - Alex's Living Room

Alex: *(to Jordan)* I can't stop thinking about it.
Jordan: Alex, relax. It's probably nothing.
Alex: But what if it's in the air? In our food?
Jordan: You're letting fear control you.
Alex: Fear or caution?

Alex stares at his untouched glass of water, feeling a chill run down his spine.

Next Morning - Alex's Bedroom

Alex: *(to himself)* I didn't sleep. I couldn't.

Alex's Phone Vibrates

[News Alert]: *Water Contamination Alert Lifted - False Alarm*

Alex: *(to Jordan)* It's over. It was nothing.
Jordan: See? Told you.
Alex: Yeah, but... the fear is still here.

Alex gazes out the window, the world looking different, more menacing than before.

10

Avalanche

The Ascent

In the quiet, I often found solace, a gentle companion in the vastness of my thoughts. But as the plane ascended, slicing through the cold, unforgiving sky, I felt the quiet morphing, twisting into a suffocating silence. I gazed out the window, watching the clouds swirl like angry spirits, and a shiver crept down my spine.

The trip was supposed to be an escape, a chance to confront the fears that had long shackled me. My therapist said it would be good for me, to face the open sky, to feel small yet unconfined. But as the plane's engines hummed a lullaby of false security, I couldn't shake the feeling of an impending, inescapable trap.

The Resort

The mountain resort was a picture of serene isolation, nestled in a world of white. I tried to lose myself in its beauty, in the endless expanse of snow and sky. But the beauty was a cruel mirage, hiding the reality of what lay beneath – a world where one could easily be swallowed, forgotten.

I joined a group of enthusiastic skiers, their laughter a stark contrast to the drumming of my heart. We were to ski down a trail, a supposedly safe path, but my mind whispered tales of those who'd been taken by the mountain, buried alive under the unforgiving snow.

The Descent

The descent began as a dance with danger, each turn a flirtation with the abyss. I tried to focus on the rhythm of my skis, but my mind betrayed me, painting vivid images of being trapped, encased in a frozen tomb.

Then it happened.

A sound, a deep, rumbling growl from the belly of the mountain, and the world turned white. I was tossed, thrown like a ragdoll in a maelstrom of snow and fear. As the avalanche consumed everything, I felt the earth swallow me, the cold seeping into my bones, a cruel echo of the grave.

The Burial

Darkness. A word too simple to describe the complete absence of light, the suffocating weight of the snow. I was conscious, yet trapped in a limbo between life and death. Every breath was a battle, each inhale a diminishing hope.

Time lost meaning. In my icy prison, I faced the core of my fear – not of death, but of being forgotten, buried alive with no one to hear my silent screams. The mountain, a colossal tombstone, stood as a sentinel over my unseen grave.

The Survival

I don't know how long I was buried before the faint sounds reached me. Rescue or delusion, I couldn't tell. But with each scrape and distant call, a spark of hope flickered in the dark.

When they finally pulled me from the snow's embrace, the world seemed too bright, too loud. But the air, the sweet, life-giving air, was a symphony to my lungs.

I had faced my deepest fear, not conquered, but endured. And in that endurance, I found a fragile strength, a whisper of survival in the face of the unrelenting mountain.

11

Veil of the Unseen Needle

The Announcement

I remember the day the pandemic was declared. Television screens flickered with images of masked faces and empty streets, a somber symphony of fear and uncertainty. But amid the chaos, one detail latched onto my psyche with a grip so tight, it felt like claws sinking into flesh: the solution, they said, would come in the form of a needle.

I've lived my life in the shadows of an unspoken terror, a fear so potent it turns my veins to ice. Needles. Just the thought sends a shiver down my spine, a primal dread that clenches my stomach in a vice. I've danced around this fear, hidden it under layers of excuses and avoidance. But now, it seems the world is conspiring to bring my deepest nightmare to the surface.

I sit in my apartment, the walls feeling closer than ever, the news blaring from the TV. "Mass vaccinations," they announce. "The only way to combat the virus." My heart races, thudding against my ribcage like a caged animal desperate to escape. I try to breathe, to find that sliver of rationality, but it's drowned out by the echo of my pounding heart.

The Escalation

Days turn into weeks, and the world outside transforms. People speak of hope, of a return to normalcy. But for me, the world has never felt more alien, more threatening. Friends and family discuss their vaccination appointments with casual ease, unaware of the storm raging inside me.

I venture out for essentials, each trip a gauntlet of anxiety. Posters line the streets, showing smiling faces and rolled-up sleeves, the sharp glint of a needle ever-present. I feel eyes on me, judging, questioning why I remain unvaccinated. The pressure builds, a suffocating weight pressing down on me.

In the solitude of my home, I am haunted by visions of the needle. It's there when I close my eyes, a sharp, menacing specter lurking in the darkness of my mind. Sleep becomes elusive, a cruel game of hide and seek where rest is always just out of reach.

The Breaking Point

The pandemic rages on, but a new battle brews within me. My phone rings; it's my sister. "Have you scheduled your vaccination yet?" she asks gently, but her words feel like daggers. I stammer, weave tales of waiting for the right time, but the truth remains unspoken, a dark secret held close to my chest.

I can't escape it anymore. The world is moving on, arms bared and fears conquered, while I remain a prisoner of my own terror. The images of needles invade my dreams, turning them into nightmares that leave me gasping for air in the dead of night.

In a moment of desperation, I reach out to a therapist, a voice of reason in the chaos of my mind. But the journey is long and fraught with shadows. Each step towards confronting my fear feels like walking through a minefield, where every thought could trigger an explosion of panic.

The Invisible Enemy

I sit in the therapist's office, the words spilling out of me like a dam bursting. The fear, the nightmares, the suffocating pressure - it all pours out. She listens, her eyes a calm harbor in the storm of my emotions.

"We'll tackle this together," she says, her voice a lifeline thrown into the turbulent sea of my thoughts. "Your fear is valid, but it doesn't have to define you."

Therapy is a dance, two steps forward, one step back. We dissect my fear, lay it bare under the scrutiny of reason and understanding. It's a monster of my own making, fed by years of avoidance and silence. But as we shine a light on it, the monster begins to lose its power, its form becoming less terrifying, more manageable.

A Glimmer of Hope

The pandemic has left its mark on the world, but it has also reshaped me. I stand outside the vaccination center, my heart still racing, but no longer out of control. I've faced my fear in the confines of therapy, but now I confront it in the real world.

The needle is there, as sharp and frightening as ever. But I'm no longer facing it alone. My therapist's words echo in my mind, a mantra of strength and courage. I step forward, my fear with me, but no longer leading me.

12

The Cloud of Success

The Inheritance

In the heart of a bustling city, where skyscrapers kissed the clouds and the streets echoed with unending life, there stood an opulent, albeit increasingly desolate, mansion. It belonged to Julian, a young heir to a colossal fortune, widely known as a 'Nepo baby', a term tossed around in both envy and scorn. The mansion, once a hive of extravagant parties and laughter, now lay silent, its echoes fading like the remnants of a forgotten dream.

Julian, with his tousled hair and eyes reflecting a brewing storm, sat alone in the grand living room. The walls, adorned with expensive art, seemed to mock him with their permanence. His parents, once titans of industry, had left him a legacy that was both a blessing and a curse. The curse, however, weighed heavier. The fortune that cushioned his life was dwindling, nibbled away by a lifestyle that knew no bounds.

Th Gilded Cage

As days merged into nights, Julian found himself increasingly confined within the walls of his mansion. The outside world, with its demands and expectations, seemed like a distant land. Friends, once numerous and ever-present, had become memories, fading with each passing day of isolation.

The mere thought of stepping into his parents' shoes, of diving into the corporate world, sent shivers down his spine. It wasn't just apprehension; it was an all-consuming dread. The offices, the meetings, the decisions that affected thousands – they were like chains, invisible yet palpable, that threatened to bind him forever.

The Memories

Julian's days were haunted by memories of his parents – their charisma, their effortless command over rooms filled with eager listeners. In contrast, Julian felt like a shadow, a mere whisper of their legacy. His attempts to engage with the business were sporadic and half-hearted, each more draining than the last. The stacks of unread emails and unreturned calls piled up like a testament to his inertia.

His only solace was the mansion, his sanctuary, where he could hide from the world's prying eyes. But even within these walls, the whispers of expectation and judgment found their way, creeping through the cracks, reminding him of his failures.

The Breaking Point

One evening, as the sun dipped below the horizon, painting the sky in shades of fire and ash, Julian stood by the window, his reflection a ghostly image against the glass. The phone rang, its shrill tone slicing through the silence. It was the board of directors – another meeting, another decision, another reminder of his inadequacy.

The room seemed to spin, the walls closing in. He could hear his heartbeat, loud and erratic, a drumbeat to his mounting panic. The weight of the name he carried, the legacy he was expected to uphold, felt like a noose around his neck.

The Embrace

In the darkest hour of the night, Julian made a choice. He would not be a puppet, dancing to the tunes of a world he never fit into. The mansion, his cage of gold and loneliness, would be his world. He decided to let go of the empire, to live in the shadows of what could have been.

The decision brought a twisted peace, a surrender to the fear that had gnawed at his soul. As he wandered through the empty halls, a smile, faint and melancholic, touched his lips. In the embrace of the shadows, Julian found his freedom, a freedom tinged with the bittersweet taste of defeat.

13

Kaleidoscope of Terror

The Vibrant Prison

The world outside had always been too vivid for me, an assault of colors that set my nerves on edge. But here, in the heart of the carnival, it was a nightmare painted in a thousand hues. I had come to confront my fear, to immerse myself in the very thing that sent shivers down my spine: Chromophobia, a relentless dread of color.

The fun house seemed innocuous at first, a whimsical labyrinth of mirrors and laughter. Yet, as I delved deeper, the air grew thick with a spectrum of colors so intense it felt like wading through a sea of living, breathing rainbows. Every wall, every mirror reflected a new shade, a new tint that made my heart race and my breath catch.

I stumbled through corridors of dizzying patterns, my fear amplifying with each turn. The sound of the carnival outside was a distant echo, replaced by the pulsing of my own heart in my ears. My footsteps echoed in the empty space, a lonely drumbeat in a world that felt too much like a vivid trap.

Reflections of Fear

The mirrors distorted more than just my reflection; they twisted my fear into grotesque shapes. My face appeared and reappeared in a myriad of colors, each more unsettling than the last. I reached out to a reflection, my hand trembling, only to recoil as if burned. The colors seemed to mock me, dancing around in a macabre waltz of hues.

I tried to close my eyes, to shut out the overwhelming flood of colors, but they pressed against my eyelids like relentless waves. The laughter of the carnival, once merry, now seemed to taunt me, a reminder of a world I couldn't escape.

The air grew thick, almost tangible, as if the colors themselves were trying to smother me. I gasped for breath, feeling as though each inhale drew more of the vibrant terror into my lungs.

The Heart of the Maze

Lost and disoriented, I found myself in the heart of the fun house – a room where the colors converged into a maelstrom of fear. The walls pulsed with light, throwing shades in every direction. I felt the panic rise like bile in my throat, threatening to overwhelm me.

In this chamber, my fear was no longer abstract. It was a living entity, wrapping its vivid tendrils around me. The colors whispered secrets I couldn't understand, secrets that spoke of an endless, chromatic abyss.

I sank to my knees, my hands clamped over my eyes. The colors, however, were not deterred. They seeped through my fingers, filling my mind with their bright, unyielding presence.

Fading into Silence

It was then, in my darkest moment, that I saw it – a sliver of darkness. A gap in the riot of color, a promise of respite. With every ounce of strength I had left, I crawled towards it, towards the absence of color that beckoned me like a beacon in the night.

The darkness enveloped me, a soothing balm against the relentless assault of the spectrum. Here, in this shadow, I found my breath, my sanity. The colors receded, their whispers fading into silence.

I emerged from the fun house with a new understanding of my fear. It would always be there, lurking in the vibrancy of the world, but I had faced it. I had walked through a kaleidoscope of terror and found my way out, not unscathed, but stronger for it.

14
The Storm

The Forsaken Shore

Amidst the cerulean embrace of the sea, the island emerged like a forgotten dream, veiled in mist and mystery. Julia and Michael, a young couple in search of adventure, never anticipated that their wanderlust on the luxurious cruise would lead them to such an eerie detour.

The tour had promised an experience of a lifetime – a visit to a secluded island, untouched by the claws of modern civilization. Yet, as their feet sank into the damp, unfamiliar sands of the shore, a sense of foreboding clung to them like the salty sea breeze.

As the day meandered into dusk, the tour group gathered to return, but an uncanny turn of events unfolded. The ship, their lifeline to the world they knew, had vanished, swallowed by the horizon, leaving nothing but a vast expanse of water stretching into infinity.

Panic clawed at Julia's throat, her heart drumming a frantic rhythm. Michael, attempting to cloak his own dread with a veneer of calm, wrapped his arms around her. But his comforting embrace could not shield them from the ominous symphony that began to play in the sky.

A low rumble, distant yet distinct, whispered threats of an impending storm. Julia's breath hitched, her eyes mirroring the turmoil within. Since childhood, the mere whisper of thunder had sent shivers down her spine, a primal fear she had never outgrown. And now, here they were, marooned on an alien land, with the wrath of the heavens about to descend upon them.

As the first flicker of lightning tore through the twilight, Julia's fears materialized into a tangible horror. The sky, now a canvas of ominous clouds, roared with anger, each clap of thunder an echo of her escalating terror.

Michael, helpless against the fury of nature and the rising tide of Julia's panic, searched desperately for shelter. The island, shrouded in darkness, offered no refuge but the gnarled embrace of ancient trees and the cold comfort of rocky crevices.

With each thunderous boom, Julia's world narrowed, her entire being consumed by the cacophony of her phobia. The storm outside raged, but it was the storm within her that threatened to unravel the very fabric of her sanity.

In the heart of the tempest, on an island that time forgot, Julia and Michael faced not just the fury of nature, but the shadows of their own fears, amplified by the echoes in the storm.

The Woods

As the night deepened, its cloak enshrouding the island, Julia and Michael found themselves wandering through an ancient forest, a labyrinth of shadows and whispers. The storm, though slightly mellowed, still rumbled in the distance, a relentless reminder of their vulnerability.

Michael led the way, his eyes scanning the darkness for a safe haven. The trees, gnarled and towering, seemed to watch them, their branches swaying like the arms of spectral sentinels. In the eerie silence between the thunderclaps, the rustling leaves whispered secrets of the island, tales lost to time and tide.

Julia's mind was a tempest of fear and confusion. Each flash of lightning, brief yet blinding, painted the woods in stark, surreal strokes. The afterimages lingered on her retinas, ghostly echoes in the dark. Her astraphobia, now a living entity, coiled around her thoughts, squeezing tighter with each thunderous heartbeat.

Michael found a small cave, a hollow in the rocks that promised a modicum of shelter. As they settled into this rough refuge, the rain began to fall, a torrential downpour that drummed on the earth with a relentless rhythm. The sound was both a lullaby and a lament, a natural symphony that played on the strings of their frayed nerves.

In the cave, huddled together for warmth and comfort, they spoke in hushed tones. Michael tried to distract Julia, recounting stories of their past adventures, of sunnier days and starlit nights. But the darkness seemed to swallow his words, leaving only the raw, unspoken fears between them.

Julia, feeling the weight of the night, closed her eyes, hoping for an escape in sleep. But rest was a stranger in this realm of unrest. Her dreams, when they came, were fragmented visions, a kaleidoscope of memories and nightmares, entwined with the relentless sound of the storm.

Outside, the island breathed and stirred. Creatures, hidden denizens of this isolated world, moved in the shadows, their eyes glowing like embers in the darkness. They were the silent observers of the human drama unfolding in their midst, their presence an unseen but palpable force.

As dawn approached, the storm began to wane, its fury spent. The first light of morning filtered through the dense canopy, casting dappled patterns on the cave's threshold. Julia and Michael, wearied by the night's ordeal, greeted the new day with a cautious hope.

Yet, the island held secrets, and the daylight would unveil a new chapter in their unexpected journey. The storm had passed, but its echoes lingered, woven into the very fabric of the island and the hidden fears that lay within.

Eyes Not Seen

As the first rays of dawn pierced the gloom, Julia and Michael emerged from their rocky refuge, their bodies stiff and minds weary. The island, bathed in the soft morning light, seemed a different world from the shadowy realm of the night. Yet, the tranquility was deceptive, a thin veil over the unknown dangers lurking within.

They decided to explore the island, hoping to find a signal for help or perhaps other stranded souls. The forest, which had seemed so menacing under the cloak of darkness, now revealed its true beauty. Towering trees adorned with vibrant, exotic flowers, and the air, fresh and crisp, filled their lungs with renewed vitality.

But as they ventured deeper, a subtle sense of unease began to grow. The beauty of the island was almost surreal, too pristine, as if untouched by the hands of time. The animals, too, were strangely absent, their presence felt but not seen, as if they were mere shadows flitting between the trees.

Julia's fear, though abated, still lingered in her heart. The sky, a clear azure, held no trace of the previous night's storm, but its echoes were etched in her soul. Every rustle in the underbrush, every distant bird call, seemed to her like a harbinger of another tempest.

They stumbled upon a clearing, where the remains of an old structure lay hidden beneath overgrowth. It was a relic of a bygone era, perhaps a shelter built by former inhabitants or castaways. The sight of it reignited a flicker of hope in them – if others had survived here, so could they.

As Michael inspected the structure, Julia's gaze was drawn to the edge of the clearing. There, partially hidden by foliage, stood a statue, ancient and eroded, its features barely discernible. It was an eerie sentinel, watching over the clearing, its origins and purpose lost to time.

The day passed in a blur of exploration and discovery. They found a freshwater stream, its waters clear and cool, and fruit-bearing trees that offered sustenance. Nature, in its generous abundance, provided for their basic needs, but the luxury of safety remained elusive.

As the sun began its descent, casting long shadows across the island, a sense of urgency gripped them. They needed to find a way to signal for help, to escape this beautiful but isolating prison. They returned to the beach, scanning the horizon for any sign of a ship, any hint of rescue.

But the ocean remained empty, a vast, undulating desert, indifferent to their plight. The isolation of the island was complete, a world unto itself, with the couple as its unwilling inhabitants.

That night, as they huddled together under the stars, the unseen eyes of the island watched them, ancient and knowing. The storm had passed, but its echoes resonated in the heart of the island, a reminder of the fears and mysteries that lay hidden in its depths.

The Signal in the Sky

The days on the island melded into a surreal pattern of survival and exploration. Julia and Michael, once mere tourists, had become inhabitants of a world that oscillated between breathtaking beauty and unnerving silence.

Their daily routine revolved around gathering food, exploring the island for any signs of human life, and devising ways to signal for help. The island, though seemingly uninhabited, was a puzzle, with pieces scattered in its dense forests, mysterious ruins, and enigmatic statues.

As they adapted to their new reality, Julia's astraphobia transformed from a crippling fear to a cautious awareness. The sky, once a canvas of her deepest dread, became a source of hope and wonder. She found herself studying the clouds, discerning patterns and signs, as if the heavens might reveal their path to salvation.

Michael, ever the pragmatist, focused on building a signal fire. They chose a spot on the highest point of the island, clearing an area to create a beacon that could be seen from the sea. Gathering wood and dry brush became a daily ritual, their hopes stacked in a pyre, waiting to be ignited.

One evening, as the sun dipped below the horizon, painting the sky in hues of orange and purple, they decided it was time to light the signal fire. The match struck, a tiny flare in the twilight, and the fire caught, its flames reaching skyward like desperate fingers.

The fire crackled and roared, a bright spot in the encroaching darkness. Julia and Michael stood back, watching the flames with a mix of hope and apprehension. This fire was their message to the world, a cry for help etched in light and smoke.

As the night deepened, they kept vigil by the fire, its glow a beacon in the darkness. The stars above twinkled indifferently, the vast cosmos seemingly oblivious to their plight. Yet, in that moment, under the celestial dome, they felt a connection to something greater, an unspoken bond with the unknown.

Hours passed, and the fire began to wane, its once vigorous flames reduced to embers. Disappointment crept into their hearts, the reality of their isolation settling in like a cold shroud. But then, a flicker in the sky caught Julia's eye.

At first, she thought it was a star, but it was moving, growing brighter. A plane, distant and small, but undeniably there. They watched, breathless, as it passed over the island, a fleeting moment of connection to the world they had lost.

The plane did not stop, disappearing into the night, but its presence ignited a new flame of hope within them. They were not alone in this vast ocean; the world was out there, moving, breathing, just beyond their reach.

In the aftermath of the plane's passing, Julia and Michael sat by the dying embers of their fire, their spirits lifted. The echoes of the storm had faded, replaced by the whispers of hope and the enduring strength of human resilience.

The Heart of the Island

In the days following the sighting of the plane, Julia and Michael's resolve strengthened. The brief encounter with the outside world had rekindled their determination to escape the island's captivating yet isolating embrace.

Their efforts intensified, focusing not only on survival but on finding a more permanent way to signal for help. The idea of creating a larger, more sustainable signal fire took shape, accompanied by the construction of a makeshift raft. Every morning brought new challenges, but also new opportunities to overcome them.

As they worked, the island revealed more of its secrets. In their explorations, they stumbled upon ancient carvings on some of the trees and rocks, cryptic symbols that hinted at the island's history and its past inhabitants. These discoveries added layers of mystery and a sense of connection to the long-forgotten people who once called this place home.

Julia, whose fear of storms had once dominated her life, found a new source of strength in the very element she had feared. She began to see the storms as a natural part of the island's life, a powerful but not insurmountable force. This shift in perception marked a significant change in her, a newfound resilience forged in the crucible of their ordeal.

Their bond, too, grew stronger, the shared adversity bringing them closer in ways they had never imagined. They learned to read each other's silences and speak without words, their relationship evolving beyond the superficial ties of their previous life.

One day, while gathering wood for the signal fire, they ventured into a part of the island they had not explored before. Here, the forest gave way to a series of small cliffs overlooking the ocean. It was a breathtaking view, the vastness of the sea stretching to the horizon, a reminder of their isolation but also of the world beyond.

As they stood there, taking in the view, they noticed something unusual in the water. A current, distinct and purposeful, creating a narrow path through the waves. It was a natural phenomenon, perhaps, but to them, it seemed like a sign, a guide leading away from the island.

Emboldened by this discovery, they decided to take a risk. They would finish the raft and follow the current. It was a gamble, but one they felt compelled to take. The island had been both a sanctuary and a prison, but now it was time to leave its embrace.

The following days were a flurry of activity as they prepared for their departure. The raft was rudimentary but sturdy, built with the combined knowledge of their past and the ingenuity born of necessity.

On the morning of their departure, as they pushed the raft into the water, the island seemed to watch them, its ancient trees and hidden creatures silent witnesses to their journey. They paddled into the current, the island fading into the mists behind them.

Their future was uncertain, the ocean vast and unpredictable, but their spirits were buoyed by hope and the strength they had found in each other. The echoes of the storm had become a part of them, a reminder of their journey and the resilience of the human spirit.

As they disappeared into the horizon, the island remained, its mysteries intact, a timeless sentinel in the vast ocean, waiting for the next chapter in its eternal story.

15

The Creeping Agony

The Awakening of Pain

In the quiet recesses of my mind, a relentless throb had taken root. It was a pulsing, insidious pain, one that had crept into my consciousness slowly, insidiously, until it became a constant, unwelcome companion. My tooth, a traitor in my mouth, had become the epicenter of an agony I couldn't escape.

For years, I managed to avoid what most consider routine - a visit to the dentist. The very thought sent shivers down my spine, images of gleaming instruments and the sterile, pungent scent of medical disinfectant haunting my dreams. Even as a child, I never set foot in a dentist's office, my fear anchoring me firmly in my resolve.

But as the pain grew, so did the realization that I couldn't ignore it any longer. The toothache, once a dull, distant ache, had transformed into a sharp, constant reminder of my deepest fear. Eating became a challenge, sleep a distant memory as the throbbing in my jaw kept me awake, night after night.

The Relentless Pursuer

Days blurred into each other, each one marked by the persistent agony in my mouth. I could feel it, the infection spreading, a silent invader claiming territory within me. My face began to swell, a visible testament to the battle raging inside.

The mere idea of seeking help filled me with dread. Images of the dentist's chair, a modern-day torture device in my mind, flashed before my eyes. The sound of the drill, the sight of needles, it was all too much. The fear was so palpable, so real, it felt like an entity in itself, stalking me, gripping my heart with icy fingers.

Every mirror reflected back my growing despair. The swelling, the pain, it was all a physical manifestation of my inner turmoil. I felt trapped, cornered by my own fears, a prisoner in my body.

The Fall

The infection was winning. Fever started to set in, a constant reminder of my body's failing defenses. I knew, deep down, that this couldn't go on. I had to face my fear, but how could I? The very thought of stepping into a dentist's office made my heart race, my palms sweat.

Nightmares plagued my sleep, visions of dental instruments morphing into instruments of torture, the dentist a looming figure of dread. Each morning, I awoke with a start, the pain in my mouth a harsh return to reality.

The infection was not just in my tooth now; it had spread to my mind, coloring every thought with fear and anxiety. I felt myself spiraling, losing control, as the pain and fear became one, an indistinguishable torment.

The Decision

It was in a moment of utter despair, when the pain became unbearable, that I realized I had no choice. I had to seek help. The decision felt like a defeat, a surrender to the very thing I had spent my life avoiding.

Stepping out of my house that day, I felt like I was walking into a nightmare. Every step towards the dentist's office was a battle against my instincts to flee, to hide, to avoid the inevitable.

As I sat in the waiting room, surrounded by the very essence of my fear, I realized that this was more than just about a toothache. It was a fight against a fear that had held me captive for far too long.

CONFRONTING FEARS: A JOURNEY TOWARDS BETTER MENTAL HEALTH

The journey of confronting fears is a crucial aspect of enhancing mental health and overall well-being. Fear, a natural and powerful human emotion, plays a significant role in our survival but can also lead to persistent anxiety and avoidance behaviors when left unchecked. This article aims to explore the psychological dynamics of fear, its impact on mental health, and practical strategies for effectively confronting and managing fears.

Understanding Fear and Its Impact on Mental Health:

Fear is a response to perceived threats and can manifest in various forms, from phobias and panic attacks to generalized anxiety. It activates the body's fight-or-flight response, leading to physical symptoms like increased heart rate, sweating, and trembling. When fear becomes overwhelming or irrational, it can severely impact daily functioning and mental health. Chronic fear can lead to conditions such as anxiety disorders, depression, and post-traumatic stress disorder (PTSD).

The Role of Perception in Fear:

Perception plays a pivotal role in how we experience and respond to fear. Cognitive distortions, such as overestimating danger or underestimating one's ability to cope, can exacerbate fear. Recognizing and challenging these distorted perceptions is vital in managing fear responses.

Strategies for Confronting Fears:

1. Exposure Therapy: Gradually and systematically exposing oneself to the source of fear in a controlled environment can help reduce the fear response over time.
2. Cognitive-Behavioral Therapy (CBT): CBT focuses on changing negative thought patterns and behaviors associated with fear. It helps in developing coping strategies and resilience.
3. Mindfulness and Relaxation Techniques: Practices like meditation, deep breathing, and progressive muscle relaxation can help in managing the physiological symptoms of fear.
4. Building a Support System: Sharing fears with trusted friends, family, or support groups can provide emotional support and encouragement.
5. Professional Help: Seeking help from mental health professionals is crucial, especially for intense or persistent fears that interfere with daily life.

The Importance of Self-Compassion and Patience: Confronting fears is a gradual process that requires patience and self-compassion. It's important to acknowledge small victories and understand that setbacks are part of the journey. Self-compassion involves treating oneself with the same kindness and understanding one would offer to a friend in a similar situation.

Confronting fears is not about eliminating them entirely but learning to manage them effectively. It's a courageous step towards better mental health and a more fulfilling life. Remember, it's always okay to seek help, and taking small steps can lead to significant changes in how we perceive and handle our fears. As we learn to face our fears, we empower ourselves to live more freely and confidently, paving the way for improved mental health and overall well-being.

www.ingramcontent.com/pod-product-compliance
Lightning Source LLC
LaVergne TN
LVHW021825060526
838201LV00058B/3506